Lorene Londahl

Clues

U
La
World Geography
Famous People

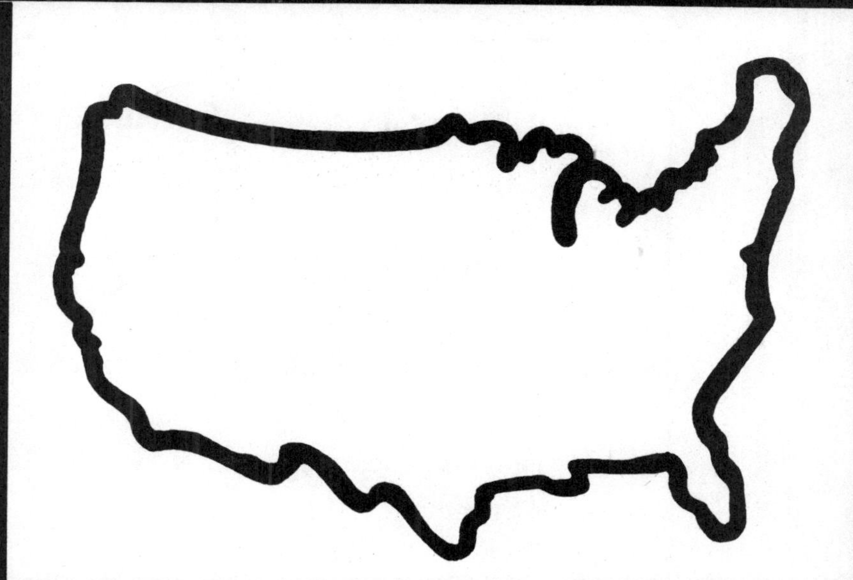

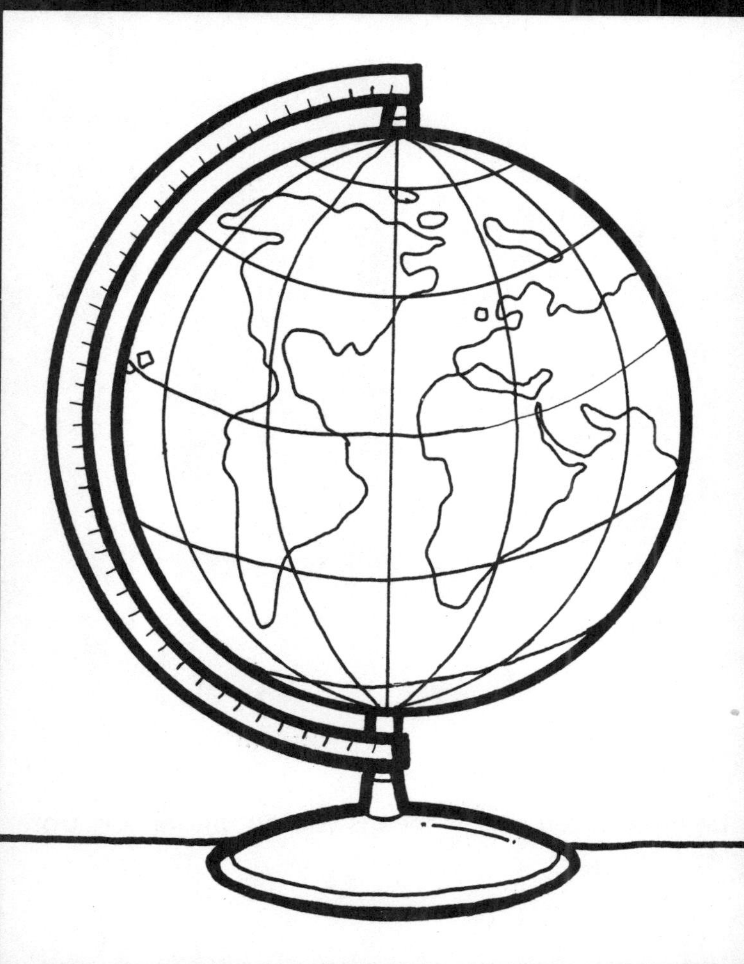

Written by Lynne Chatham

Illustrated by Annelise Palouda

Contents

Edited by **Sonsie Conroy**

Published by **Dandy Lion Publications**
P.O. Box 190
San Luis Obispo, CA 93406

Introduction

What kind of a book is *Clues?*

Clues is a collection of exercises that can be used to accomplish several goals. It is full of challenging puzzles that serve to stimulate recall of information, build deductive reasoning skills, and foster cultural and global literacy.

The exercises in this book cover four main areas — **landmarks and famous sites, U.S. geography, world geography,** and **famous people.** A companion book covers four additional topics — literature, math, logic, and things. Each section in these books contains a series of puzzles that will expose students to a wide spectrum of information.

Each exercise presents five or six clues. Students must put together the information in the clues to be able to solve the puzzle and name the person, place, or thing to which the puzzle refers. Some puzzles are quite easy. Some are quite hard. Some have clues that are direct and lead to an obvious solution, while in other puzzles students must put together the information in the clues to deduce the answer. The puzzles are meant to not just be a game of recall of trivial information but to be a forum for building thinking skills and an overview of our cultural and historical heritage.

How can I use these puzzles?

Team Play - Divide your class into groups. Give the clues, beginning with the least obvious clues, until one of the teams can give the correct answer. In order to involve all students, ask that all members of the team agree on the answer before the spokesperson for the team signals that they are ready to respond.

Weekly Challenge - Present the entire class with a different clue each day of the week. When students think they know the answer, they can submit the answer on a piece of paper. At the end of the week, report how many people guessed correctly and on which day. You can even take this information and put it into a graph. Discuss how students used the clues to solve the puzzle.

Sponge Activities - Present a puzzle when you have an extra five minutes between other classroom activities. Read all the clues to all the students. After you have read all the clues, call on individual students to give the answer. If there are no correct responses, ask students to think about and discuss the puzzle and see if they can come up with the answer later in the day. Come back to them at a later time and ask for the answer.

Research - Some of the puzzles may require students to look up information in reference books. Have an atlas, dictionary, and encyclopedia in your classroom. Encourage students to use the reference materials to decode the clues and unlock the answers.

After a puzzle has been solved, you can also use the subject of the puzzle as a topic for further investigation. While the clues present interesting facts, there are many more things to learn about the people, places or things that are presented in the puzzles. Challenge students to find out more about the subject.

Thinking Skills - Many of the puzzles (particularly in the math and logic section, but to a lesser extent in all other sections) require students to be able to infer certain information from the clues or to put together information in several clues to arrive at a correct answer. While a broad knowledge base is helpful in solving these puzzles, an ability to infer and deduce is also essential. As you work the puzzles, have students discuss the thinking strategies that allowed them to arrive at an answer.

Cooperative Learning - Divide your class into groups of five or six (depending on the number of clues for the puzzles you choose). Cut the clues in strips and give each member of the group a different clue. Students must then share their clues and work together to solve the puzzle. This approach adds the dimension of communication and teamwork as a necessity for being able to solve the puzzle. There is also a sharing of information among team members that expands the knowledge base beyond what members will know individually.

And so?

Use this book as a versatile tool. Use it as many different ways as your imagination will allow. Your students will enjoy using this book to expand their knowledge of the world around them and historical events and people, while they build important thinking skills.

1

- Once you're in Greece, find your way to Athens and look up.
- It is home to famous ancient Greek buildings.
- It was considered a sanctuary for the city's gods and the center of religious ceremonies.
- It means "high city" in Greek.
- The Parthenon sits on this famous hill.

2

- To find it you must travel to the country that is shaped like a boot.
- Continue your search in the city of Rome.
- It's big, oval-shaped and very old.
- Built in 80 AD, today only a portion of it is standing.
- In its better days it was a stadium where gladiator fights and different competitions were held.
- Today many sports arenas are named after this building.

3

- It's located in the country that lies south of Belgium.
- When you get there, be prepared to look up, because it is very tall.
- It's one of the most famous landmarks in this capital city.
- It was built in 1889 for an international exposition.
- It was named after the engineer who designed it.
- It's 984 feet tall.

4

- It's located in the Lone Star State.
- It was once a mission but is now a monument and museum.
- A historic battle waged on this spot pitted less than 200 Americans against over 4,000 Mexicans.
- Names like Davy Crockett and Jim Bowie are associated with this monument.
- It is considered the "cradle of Texas liberty."
- The battle call for Texan independence became "Remember the ______."

5

- You'll find this landmark in the northern part of a country that has a very old culture.
- It's so large that astronauts have seen it from space.
- It's over 1500 miles in length and averages 25 feet in height.
- It is the world's largest wall fortification.
- It took nearly two centuries to complete.
- You can follow it from Shanhaikuan to Chiayukuan, China.

6

- Travel first to the country that is famous for spaghetti and pizza.
- In the central part of this country you'll find a city that has the same name as this landmark.
- It was built as a bell tower for a church.
- Galileo performed a famous experiment here. He dropped a cannon ball and a feather from the top and proved that objects of different masses fall to the earth at the same speed.
- It once stood erect but only for a very short time. It began tilting before it was completed.

7

- This structure is in a large country that has a lot of monuments. This is one of the most famous.
- When you visit the country's capital, you'll have an opportunity to visit this memorial.
- It contains a statue of the person for whom it is named.
- It is a tribute to the sixteenth president.
- The person who is memorialized by this monument also has his picture on the country's smallest denomination of coin.

8

- You'll find these landmarks in a country that lies east of the Red Sea and south of the Mediterranean sea.
- Huge and made of stone, they were originally built as tombs for leaders.
- The greatest one is at Giza, near Cairo.
- All of the four sides are shaped like triangles. The base is a square.
- Other monuments like these are found in Mexico and Central America.

9

- You'll find this landmark overlooking a harbor.
- It was designed and made in France but stands in an English-speaking country.
- How would you like a birthday present like this one that is over 150 feet tall?
- This is one landmark that actually has a gender — female.
- On the right you'll see a torch, and on the left you'll find the date July IV MDCCLXXVI
- It is a symbol of freedom.

10

- It is located in a country that lies between the Bay of Bengal and the Arabian Sea.
- It was built as a memorial to a ruler's wife.
- It is considered one of the world's most beautiful buildings.
- When it was constructed in the 1600s, it took 20,000 men 11 years to complete.
- It is considered the most perfect example of Mongol-style architecture.
- This domed symmetrical building is surrounded by beautiful water gardens.

11

- This structure is considered one of the greatest engineering feats of the world.
- It is about 40 miles long.
- It has locks but no keys.
- Before it was constructed, ships had a long, dangerous journey.
- It shortened the journey from the Pacific to the Atlantic by 8,000 miles.
- It cuts through a country whose name is the same as this structure.

12

- From Ankara, Turkey, head in a northerly direction for nearly 1,000 miles.
- It was a royal palace until the early 18th century. It became governmental headquarters again in 1922.
- Within the walls are churches, four cathedrals and many palaces.
- Fortresses in many Russian medieval cities bear the same name.
- It sits adjacent to Red Square.

13

- It was one of the Seven Wonders of the Ancient World.
- It was built by Nebuchadnezzar for his wife.
- It had a series of planted terraces.
- It was located in a country that is now Iraq.
- It was located in the city that was the capital of the ancient kingdom of Babylonia.

14

- You'll find this landmark on a large island that lies to the west of the North Sea.
- It is an example of a megalithic monument.
- It was built between 1800 and 1400 B.C.
- The main structure is large and shaped like a circle.
- The pieces were used to show astronomical relationships.
- It remains one of the world's great mysteries.

15

- It's a famous fortress on the River Thames.
- It was built by William the Conquer and Henry VIII between 1078 and 1300.
- Over the years it has served as a fortress, a palace, a prison, and a mint.
- It now houses the crown jewels and an armor museum.
- It bears the name of the capital city where it is located.

16

- It is located in the United States, but it's not in any state.
- Its address is on Pennsylvania Avenue.
- The first resident was John Adams.
- The site was chosen by George Washington.
- Damaged during the War of 1812, it was rebuilt in 1818 and painted its distinctive color.
- It's the official residence of the country's highest elected official.

17

- Plato was one of the many authors who have written about this place.
- It was located between Europe and the Americas.
- It had an advanced civilization.
- No one knows what happened to it, but many believe it was destroyed by an earthquake.
- Perhaps it was just a myth.

18

- It divided a city in 1961.
- It was only 26.5 miles (43 km) long.
- It had 12 official crossings. Of these, Brandenburg was its most famous.
- It was heavily fortified and guarded.
- It came down in 1989.

19

- You'll find this landmark in London.
- It's a permanent fixture in the parliament building.
- Its name doesn't tell you that it's a clock.
- Its name tells about its size.
- Its name is a man's name.

20

- This bridge is a part of U.S. Highway 101.
- It spans the opening to the Bay of San Francisco.
- Its name refers to its location, not to its color.
- It is one of the world's most eye-catching bridges.
- It stands high so ships can pass under it.

21

- It's considered one of the most outstanding buildings of the 20th century.
- It was completed in 1973 after 14 years of construction.
- You'll find this building overlooking a busy harbor in Australia.
- It looks like a series of overlapping sails.
- Music fills its chambers.

22

- It sits on the River Seine in Paris.
- It's noted for being an excellent example of Gothic architecture.
- This famous cathedral was built in 1313.
- It has twin towers, huge flying buttresses and beautiful colored-glass windows.
- The name means "our lady" in French.

23

- It lay hidden in the jungle for over 300 years.
- It was discovered by Bingham in 1911.
- Its buildings include temples constructed of blocks of granite, some weighing more than ten tons.
- The last Inca warrior left this mountain stronghold after the Spanish conquest in the 1530s.
- It is known as the Lost City of the Incas.

24

- This monument is located in the state that is south of North Dakota.
- This famous peak is part of the Black Hills, the highest mountains east of the Rockies.
- It was created by Gutzon Borglum.
- The 60-foot portraits are a stony tribute to four great men.
- Look up and you'll see Thomas, Abraham, George and Theodore.

1

- When it's 10:00 am in New York, it's 7:00 am in this city.
- It is one of the largest cities in the U.S.
- It's south of Seattle and north of Mexico City.
- It was once an Indian village, a mission, and a Spanish outpost.
- It's known as the "City of Angels."

2

- It's a city in the second largest state in the nation.
- It sits 50 miles from the Gulf of Mexico.
- It is the fourth largest city in the U.S.
- Its wealth was built on oil.
- It is the home of the Johnson Space Center.
- It was named after the first president of the Republic of Texas.

3

- It borders two countries.
- Covering more than 32,000 square miles, it is the world's largest.
- While it's the world's largest, it does not contain the most water.
- It is nearly as large as the country of Austria.
- It is part of a series of lakes that are "great."

4

- If you travel to the south and west, you'll find this state.
- One of its borders is a foreign country.
- Oraibi (a Hopi village in this state) is the oldest continuously inhabited town in the United States.
- You'll find the Grand Canyon National Park in this state.
- It's home to several Native American tribes.
- You won't find London Bridge in London any more; you'll find it here.

5

- This state often sets records for cold weather.
- Its northern border is Canada.
- Its name comes from the Sioux word for "allies."
- Farming is the main business.
- It was part of the Dakota Territory that was divided into two states.
- You'll find the Badlands in this state.

6

- Seven of the first twelve presidents were from this state.
- Founded in 1607 by John Smith, it was the first permanent English settlement in North America.
- This is where you'll find Monticello and the Arlington National Cemetery.
- It was named for Queen Elizabeth, the Virgin Queen.
- It borders a state with a similar name.

7

- It's neither in the north, south, east or west.
- It was once a boom town.
- It's north of Santa Fe, New Mexico and east of Salt Lake City, Utah.
- It's in a state that has straight boundaries.
- It was founded during the great "Pike's Peak or Bust" gold rush.
- At an elevation of 5,280 feet above sea level, it is called the "Mile High City."

8

- Its nickname, The Evergreen State, tells about the kind of vegetation you'll find there.
- It borders the largest ocean in the world, a foreign country, and a long river.
- The highest point in the state is Mt. Rainier.
- Lewis and Clark ended their expedition here.
- A volcano erupted here in 1980.
- It was named after a famous president.

9

- It is one of the longest rivers in North America.
- It is also known as Rio Bravo del Norte.
- It flows eastward.
- It begins in Colorado and ends its journey in the Gulf of Mexico.
- It forms an international boundary.

10

- It is approximately 1,800 miles in length, stretching from Newfoundland to Alabama.
- Bring your shovel and maybe you can dig up some iron and coal.
- It includes names like Blue Ridge, Smokey, White, Allegheny, and Cumberland.
- The highest point is Mt. Mitchell.
- It was an early day barrier to westward movement.
- It is home to the longest marked hiking trail in the world.

11

- From Hawaii, head north.
- They separate the Bering Sea from the Pacific Ocean.
- The chain is made of over 150 separate pieces formed by volcanoes.
- If you like to fish, this is the place to go.
- They are part of the largest state.
- They were discovered in 1741 by Vitus Bering, claimed by Russia, and purchased by the U.S. in 1867.

12

- From Illinois, travel south. From Texas, travel east.
- It was one of the six original states of the Confederacy in the Civil War.
- It was the home of Jefferson Davis, the first president of the Confederacy.
- The 35° north latitude forms its northern border.
- At one time "cotton was king," but now other crops are raised here.
- Its name is a favorite word for young people to spell because of the repetition of letter patterns.

13

- History happened here — a famous tea party and a shot heard around the world.
- It was home to many famous people including John Adams, John F. Kennedy, and Paul Revere.
- It has many small harbors and a famous cape shaped like a fish hook.
- Ranking 45th in size and 11th in population, this is one of the most densely populated states.
- It is bordered by two small states to the north, two small states to the south, and the Atlantic Ocean to the east.

14

- It's located in a state that is bordered by the Gulf of Mexico and the Atlantic Ocean.
- Lake Okeechobee sits at the northern end.
- You'll find an abundance of wildlife and plants here.
- It's the third largest national park.
- The average elevation is sea level.
- Some of the inhabitants have large, powerful jaws.

15

- From Wisconsin you can travel east or north.
- It has two parts, separated by a body of water.
- Henry Ford changed the state.
- It borders four of the Great Lakes.
- Whether you drive a Chevrolet, a Ford or a Chrysler, you'll feel at home in this state.

16

- It starts in Alaska and terminates in Mexico.
- Rivers begin here and either flow west to the Pacific or east to the Atlantic.
- It's the birthplace of the Rio Grande, Missouri, Columbia, and Colorado, to name a few.
- It encompasses the Glacier, Yellowstone and Grand Teton National Parks.
- The highest point is Mt. Elbert in Colorado.
- It is the continental divide.

17

- Located on the Mississippi River, it is an international port.
- It boasts a rich blend of several cultures — it has been under both French and Spanish rule.
- It became part of the United States as a result of the Louisiana Purchase.
- If you like big parties, come here for Mardi Gras.
- It is the home of Dixieland jazz.
- It's one of those "new" cities.

18

- It is the largest in area and the smallest in population.
- About one quarter of it lies north of the Arctic Circle.
- Here you'll find the highest mountain in North America.
- If you want to find oil, look on the North Slope.
- Its name comes from an Aleutian word meaning "great lands."
- It includes the most northerly and most westerly points.

19

- It was first settled by Indian nations forced out of the South Atlantic by the Indian Removal Act .
- It is located on the banks of the Arkansas River in a state with a panhandle.
- The discovery of oil made it the "Oil Capital of the World."
- The name is a corruption of the word "Tullahassee," meaning old town.
- This city's history is a blend of oil barons and Indian culture.
- Try to come to the big powwow held here each summer.

20

- This state was independent for nearly ten years before being annexed to the United States in 1845.
- Its borders include a foreign country and a large, well-known river.
- It is bigger than most of the states, but it's not the biggest.
- It has several ports on the Gulf of Mexico.
- One lone star flies over this state.

21

- It is the oldest and largest national park.
- It is considered a geological wonderland.
- You can find hot springs, mud pools, geysers and petrified forests here.
- Most of it is in northwest Wyoming.
- They say you can set your watch by Old Faithful.

22

- It is located on land ceded by Maryland in 1790.
- Designed by Pierre L'Enfant, it was the first carefully planned capital.
- If you visit, you can throw a stone into the Potomac River.
- It is a city of monuments and museums.
- This city has the same boundaries as the federal district in which it is located.
- It is named after the president who chose the site upon which it was built.

23

- It's one of the largest cities in the country.
- It was first named New Amsterdam but was renamed by the British in 1664.
- One of its five parts is the island of Manhattan.
- It was allegedly purchased from natives for $24 worth of goods.
- You'll find Wall Street, Harlem, Greenwich Village, and the Hudson River here.
- A center for trade, finance, and communications, it is known as the Big Apple.

24

- It is a mile deep and over 200 miles long.
- The landscape of exposed rock was created by the Colorado River.
- It took 21 million years to get to its present form.
- Part of its name describes its size.
- It's like taking a geological time trip.
- If you want to visit, you'll have to travel to Arizona.

1

- It's an island continent.
- It is situated between the Indian and Pacific Oceans.
- It has an abundance of marsupial mammals and animals such as the anteater and platypus.
- Its first inhabitants arrived by boat from Southeast Asia.
- Its land area is slightly less than that of the United States.
- Along the coast you can see the world's largest coral reef, the Great Barrier Reef.

2

- This country is located on the South American continent.
- It is on the eastern coast.
- The capital of this country is a planned city with a name that echoes the name of the country.
- The official language of this country is Portuguese.
- The largest cities in this country are São Paulo and Rio de Janeiro.
- It is the largest country on the continent.

3

- It is one of the Scandinavian countries.
- Its early inhabitants were called Vikings.
- It was ruled by Denmark and Sweden before it finally gained independence in 1905.
- This country is known for its picturesque coastline that features fjords and many islands.
- Sweden is to the south and Finland is to the east.
- It extends farther north than any of its neighboring countries.

4

- The 80° north latitude runs through this country.
- It's an island in the North Atlantic Ocean that lies partially within the Arctic Circle.
- Its name does not describe its landscape.
- It's closer to Canada than to its mother country, Denmark.
- It was discovered by the Norwegian explorer, Eric the Red.
- It is the largest island in the world.

5

- To find this place, set sail for northern Africa.
- It's very hot, dry and windy.
- Covering three and one half million square miles, it's considered the biggest and greatest.
- Though it is constantly changing shape, it stretches from the Atlantic Ocean to the Red Sea.
- Though it is largely hot and dry, it contains many oases.
- It covers several countries.

6

- You'll find this small island in the South Pacific.
- Look 2,000 miles west of Chile and 1,000 miles east of Pitcairn Island.
- One of the ancient mysteries of the world is on this island.
- Some of the inhabitants are made of stone.
- It is a Chilean historic monument.
- It takes its name from the day it was discovered, a special spring holiday.

7

- Bring your overcoat; it's very, very cold here.
- It was finally "conquered" in 1953.
- It is the tallest and most inaccessible in the world, making it the ultimate climber's challenge.
- It is named for the person who discovered it in 1856.
- It straddles the border between Nepal and Tibet.
- It is a part of the Himalayan mountain chain.

8

- It is a famous city in the country that's shaped like a boot.
- It sits at the very northern end of the Adriatic Sea.
- It is considered a marvel of Renaissance architecture and engineering.
- In the beginning it was just a series of tiny islands.
- If you go there, better bring a boat rather than a car.
- Its famous canals are its streets.

9

- They call it a sea but it is really a large lake.
- With over 12 million tons of salt, it is the saltiest sea.
- The River Jordan flows into it but there is not outlet.
- This sea lies approximately 1,300 feet (393 meters) below sea level.
- Ownership is divided between Jordan and Israel.
- Its name denotes the fact that nothing can live in it.

10

- At over 4,100 miles, it is the longest of its kind.
- It starts in central Africa and ends in the Mediterranean Sea.
- It has two branches with the same name, the White ____ and the Blue ____.
- It is about 150 miles longer than the Amazon.
- The Aswan High Dam harnesses its power.
- Its annual overflow has helped Egyptian agriculture throughout history.

11

- These are one of the many groups of islands in the Pacific Ocean.
- Start in Ecuador and follow the equator west.
- Charles Darwin explored these islands in 1831.
- One of the attractions here is the unusual animals.
- The islands were named after the giant turtles found there.
- The group of islands is a national park and wildlife sanctuary.

12

- If you want to set sail, you can choose either the Persian Gulf or the Red Sea.
- It is bordered by eight smaller countries, and it occupies 4/5 of a large peninsula.
- Its main resource is its rich oil fields.
- If you want to travel to Mecca, you'll have to come to this country.
- Mohammed, the prophet of Islam, began the unification of this country in A.D. 622, and the modern country was united by Ibn Saud in 1953.

13

- It is the capital of a country that has the same name.
- It is one of the most populous cities in the world.
- It sits atop a plateau at an altitude of over 7,000 feet.
- It is on the site of the old Aztec capital of Tenochtitlan.
- For over 300 years it was the capital of the Spanish colonies in the New World.
- Spanish is the language that most of these city-dwellers speak.

14

- This country has one of the world's largest populations — about 20% of the world's people.
- It remained in self-imposed isolation from the rest of the world until the late 1970s.
- Marco Polo was an early visitor to this Asian country.
- If you're looking for the Yangtze, you'll find it here.
- Its modern history began in 1949 with Mao Tse-tung.
- If you lived in this country you would probably speak Mandarin.

15

- It lies along the Pacific coast of South America.
- The driest place in the world (the Atacama Desert) is in this country.
- If you're in Santiago, you're in the capital.
- Look around you and you'll find Peru, Bolivia, and Argentina.
- The Andes Mountains stretch along the eastern border.

16

- It was originally known as Rupert's Land and was once owned by the Hudson's Bay Company.
- The Rockies rise high and rugged in the southwestern corner.
- It is the westernmost prairie province.
- It is known for its long, cold winters.
- Banff and Jasper National Parks are found in this province.
- It is Canada's leading producer of petroleum.

17

- If you're in the Caribbean, stop by this group of islands.
- From Puerto Rico, head east.
- These islands were discovered by Columbus in 1493.
- Ownership is shared between the United States and Britain.
- There are about a hundred small islands. Three of the larger islands are named after saints.
- If you want to live in a city, one of your few choices would be Charlotte Amalie.

18

- It is east of Munich and west of Budapest
- This famous city sits on the Danube River.
- It was home to several renowned musicians like Mozart, Beethoven, Brahms, and Strauss.
- It was capital of the Austro-Hungarian Empire until 1918.
- German is the favored language.
- This capital city is about 750 miles east of the capital of France.

19

- To reach this location, you must first travel to the continent of Africa.
- Then head your boat up the Zambezi River.
- You'll find this famous place between Zimbabwe and Zambia.
- With a drop of 400 feet, it is one of the world's more famous waterfalls.
- It was named after an English queen.

20

- This country is the most densely populated country in North Africa.
- It is much smaller than its other North African neighbors.
- It is bordered by the Mediterranean Sea, Algeria and Libya.
- You'll find both the Atlas Mountains and the Sahara Desert in this country.
- Petroleum is an important resource.
- The capital city is the site of ancient Carthage, a city founded by the Phoenicians.

21

· This city was founded in the 12th century and named Edo.
· Over the years it has been damaged by earthquakes, fire and war.
· The city is located in an island nation in the South Pacific.
· To the south is Mt. Fuji.
· It is located on Honshu Island.
· It is the capital and largest city of a country that is a small but important world power.

22

· With an average altitude of 12,000 feet, it is known as the "Roof of the World."
· It is an autonomous region of China.
· The Himalayan Mountains can be found in this country.
· The Dalai Lama is the secular and religious leader of the people in this country.
· It is surrounded by Burma, India, Nepal, Bhutan and Sikkim.
· The country is also called the "Land of the Lamas."

23

· It is known as the "Eternal City."
· The Tiber River flows through this ancient city in central Italy.
· It is famous for the Forum, the Vatican, the Colosseum, and St. Peter's.
· Legend tells of the city being founded by Romulus and Remus in 735 B.C.
· In ancient times it was the center of an empire that extended beyond the boundaries of Italy.
· It is the capital city.

24

· Thirty-eight percent of this country is below sea level.
· It borders the North Sea.
· Its important cities include Amsterdam and The Hague.
· It is bordered by Belgium and Germany.
· The people in this country speak Dutch.
· It once had an empire that included holdings in Indonesia, Africa, the West Indies and America.

25

- This country is located in the South Pacific.
- It is a country of two main islands and many smaller islands.
- It is very mountainous.
- Its closest neighbor is another English-speaking country.
- It is the home to many rare birds, including the kiwi.
- A progressive country, it was the first in the world to give women the right to vote in 1893.

26

- It is a city that occupies both an island and its adjoining mainland.
- It is a major world center for trade in the Far East.
- The official languages are English and Chinese.
- It came into England's hands in 1841.
- It will return to Chinese sovereignty in 1997 under a "One Country, Two Systems" arrangement.
- It lies south of Canton in the South China Sea.

27

- It overlooks the Pacific Ocean.
- Here you'll find Lake Titicaca, the highest lake in the world.
- The Orinoco, the São Francisco, and the Amazon originate here.
- It is one of the world's longest and highest mountain ranges.
- Aconcagua is the highest peak.
- It is called the backbone of South America.

28

- It was first discovered by Diaz in 1488, who named it Cape of Storms.
- It presented obstacles for sailors who tried to sail around it.
- Vasco da Gama first sailed around it in 1498.
- It is the tip of a continent in the southern hemisphere.
- Its real name is Cape Province.
- It is bordered by the Indian Ocean and the Atlantic Ocean.

29

- It is a city of canals.
- It began as a medieval fishing village but is now a major European commercial port.
- It has been called the "Venice of the North."
- This port is linked to the North Sea by a large canal.
- It is 365 miles west of Berlin.
- It is the capital and largest city of a country where people speak Dutch.

30

- It is the political, cultural and commercial capital of one of the world's largest and most populous countries.
- It was laid out by Kublai Khan in the 13th century.
- It is comprised of two walled sections — the Inner and the Outer Cities.
- It is located very close to the 40° north latitude.
- The splendors of this city were described in Marco Polo's writings.

31

- It is located in southeast Asia and lies south of China.
- It is wedged between Cambodia, Burma and Laos.
- To the south is a gulf with the same name as this country.
- It used to be called Siam.
- Bangkok is its major port
- It is located on both the Indochinese and Malayan Peninsulas.

32

- It is not the longest in the world.
- It is considered sacred.
- Some people believe that it is the reincarnation of the goddess Ganga.
- Pilgrims travel to bathe in its waters for purification.
- It begins in the Himalayas and ends in the Bay of Bengal.

1

- He was premier of one of the world's largest and most powerful countries, but his impact was felt outside of his country.
- He was responsible for *glasnost* (openness) and *perestroika* (restructuring) and arms reduction.
- He was a 20th century Soviet leader.
- He led the change from communism to democracy and capitalism.
- In the end, he was out of a job.

2

- He was an important inventor in the 1800s.
- He was an educator of the deaf.
- He lived before call-waiting and car phones.
- He founded a large communications company that bore his name.
- His greatest invention is something you use every day to communicate with other people.
- Another invention went around and around and produced sound.

3

- An American who was born and lived in the South, this person affected the entire nation.
- He was a minister and more.
- His dream inspired many people.
- He advocated protest by passive resistance.
- He led the civil rights movement that sought to do away with segregation and racial injustice.
- He won the Nobel Prize in 1964 and was assassinated in 1968.

4

- This composer began composing music when he was only five years old.
- He called Austria home.
- During his short life he became one of the greatest classical composers.
- By the age of four, he was touring Europe and giving concerts.
- You might not like to have a first name of Wolfgang, but he probably didn't think it was strange.
- He wrote over 600 musical pieces, one being the opera *The Magic Flute.*

5

- If you're looking for someone to paint your picture, he would be the best.
- His native language was Dutch.
- You'd have to travel back to the 17th century to meet him.
- While a lot of famous people are known by their last names, he is known best by his first name.
- One of his most famous paintings is *The Night Watch.*
- He was one of the world's greatest artists.

6

- He was a diplomat, philosopher, writer, inventor and scientist during the 1700s.
- Just because he wrote *Poor Richard's Almanac,* don't think that his name was Richard.
- His experiment proved that lightning was electricity.
- He invented bifocal glasses and an efficient stove that bears his name.
- He helped draft a document that declared the independence of his country from its mother country across the Atlantic and also helped draft his country's first constitution.

7

- His talents extended to architecture, politics, science, invention and writing.
- He was one of the principle writers of the document that declared the independence of his country from its mother country across the Atlantic.
- His biggest purchase was the Louisiana Purchase.
- He was his country's third president.
- His home, Monticello, is a popular tourist spot.

8

- He went a long way for a boy with only a little formal schooling.
- A politician, he eventually took his country's highest office.
- When things in his country were falling part, he worked to keep the country united.
- If you're looking through his papers, you'll find the Emancipation Proclamation and the Gettysburg Address.
- Pick up a penny and you'll find his face.

9

- He flew higher than most pilots.
- His aircrafts were called *Gemini* and *Apollo*.
- In 1969 he walked where no one had walked before.
- He worked for NASA when he achieved his greatest accomplishment.
- His famous words compared a small step and a giant leap.

10

- Music was his thing.
- He lived in Germany in the 1700s and 1800s.
- He was one of the world's greatest composers.
- He continued to compose music even after he became deaf.
- You might call it a song for moonlight; he called it *Moonlight Sonata*.
- Every young piano student has learned to play his "Ode to Joy."

11

- Despite his lack of formal education, he became one of the greatest inventors of the late 1800s and early 1900s.
- With over 1,000 patents, he was the most productive inventor of his time.
- He perfected the phonograph.
- Every time you turn on a light, you can thank this person.
- Many electric companies still bear his name.

12

- He lived during the late 1400s and early 1500s but he was ahead of his time.
- He was one of those talented Italians.
- He has been called the epitome of the "Renaissance Man."
- His *Mona Lisa* is one of his most famous paintings.
- Not only an artist, he was also a scientist, sculptor, engineer, architect and inventor.
- His last name is the same as the Italian town in which he was born, Vinci.

13

- He was leader of one of the world's largest and most populous countries.
- He defeated the Nationalists under Chiang Kai-shek in 1949 and ruled until his death in 1976.
- He was the founder of the People's Republic of China.
- He launched the "Cultural Revolution."
- He was commonly known as "Chairman."

14

- This important scientist was born in Germany and later moved to the United States.
- He won the Nobel Prize in 1921.
- He provided proof that matter is made of atoms.
- His theory of relativity made a dramatic impact on the world of physics.
- He is most famous for $E = mc^2$
- Though he advocated the development of the atomic bomb, he also supported world peace.

15

- He was an Italian scientist during the 16th century.
- He made the first complete astronomical telescope.
- He supported the theory that the sun was the center of the solar system.
- He developed the formula for the swing of a pendulum.
- He showed that bodies of unequal weight will fall to earth at the same velocity.
- Through he is usually refered to by his first name only, he had a last name, Galilei.

16

- He was a 19th century naturalist.
- His scientific expedition began when he boarded the *HMS Beagle* for a trip around the world.
- His theory of natural selection made him famous.
- He thought that both plants and animals were in a constant state of evolution.
- If you want to know the "Origin of Species," ask this person.
- His theories were opposed on religious grounds and caused heated arguments.

17

- He was an explorer from Venice, Italy during the 13th and 14th centuries.
- He was the first European to travel across all of Asia, and he returned to Venice from his travels with many treasures.
- He inspired explorers to find a route to the East.
- He wrote about his adventures in a book entitled *Travels.*
- He traveled to China to the court of the great Kublai Khan between 1271 and 1295.

18

- He lived and worked in Florence and Rome during the 15th and 16th centuries.
- He was an Italian artist, sculptor, architect and poet.
- He is considered the artistic genius of the Renaissance.
- His famous works include the Sistine Chapel and the rebuilding of St. Peter's Basilica.
- He is one of the world's most famous artists; so famous that you need only refer to him by one name.

19

- She was born in England in 1820.
- Her nickname was "Lady with the Lamp."
- She worked during the Crimean War.
- She was the founder of modern nursing.
- Her last name is the same as a songbird that sings at night.

20

- She was an American author and social worker.
- She overcame physical handicaps to become a distinguished scholar and lecturer.
- The play and movie *The Miracle Worker* highlights the work of her tutor and friend, Anne Sullivan, who helped her overcome her handicaps.
- She lost her sight, hearing and ability to speak at an early age.
- She spent a large part of her life working for support and programs for handicapped people.

21

- He was one of the world's greatest military commanders in ancient history.
- He became king of Macedonia at the age of 20.
- His kingdom grew to be the largest that the world had ever known.
- His goal was to conquer the world.
- He lived between 356 and 323 B.C.
- He will go down in history as "great" if not the greatest.

22

- He was a statesman, soldier and author.
- He lived and worked in England, but he influenced the whole world.
- He mobilized Britain during World War II with "blood, toil, tears, and sweat."
- He won the Nobel Prize for literature in 1953.
- He coined the phrase "iron curtain" while warning western nations about communist expansion.
- He is probably best noted for being England's prime minister during World War II.

23

- She was a scientist at a time when there were few women in science.
- She won the Nobel Prize for physics in 1903 and for chemistry in 1911.
- She discovered two radioactive elements — radium and polonium.
- She lived and worked in France.
- Her last name is the name of a unit of measure for the activity of radioactive substances. The symbol for this unit is Ci.

24

- She was born in the land of the free, but she was not free.
- She worked for a railroad that was secretive.
- She was an underground conductor and an abolitionist.
- Her code name was "Moses."
- During the Civil War she was a spy and scout.
- Over 300 people owed their freedom to her.

25

- He was a Viking who lived in the tenth century.
- He traveled across the Atlantic Ocean before other people were making such journeys.
- He was on a journey to bring Christianity to Greenland when he got blown off course.
- He founded the colonies of Woodland and Vinland (possibly Maryland and Newfoundland).
- His father's name was Eric the Red, who explored and colonized Greenland.

26

- Two people did the work and shared the honors.
- It started with bicycles but moved on to another form of transportation.
- History was made at Kitty Hawk.
- In this case, two heads were better than one.
- They changed the way people got from here to there.

27

- He established the Peace Corps and a domestic program called the "New Frontier."
- Though he was elected for four years, he only served two years.
- He was the youngest president.
- His tensest moment was the Cuban Missile Crisis.
- His most famous quote is, "Ask not what your country can do for you. Ask what you can do for your country."

28

- She was a French peasant girl until the voices she heard led her on a mission to save her country.
- She is a national heroine in France and there is a national holiday in her honor.
- She lead French armies against the English in the Hundred Years' War.
- She was also known as the Maid of Orleans.
- She was finally burned as a heretic and witch by the English.

29

- He was a famous French general and emperor during the early 1800s.
- He was considered a military genius.
- French law is still based on his codes.
- He dissolved the Holy Roman Empire and ruled over most of the continent.
- He ruled until he met his Waterloo.
- He sold the Louisiana Territory to the United States for 15 million dollars.

30

- He was known as the father of his country because he lead it to independence.
- He was known as Mahatma, which means "Great Lord."
- He advocated nonviolent resistance to British rule.
- He was a model of moral life to the people in India.
- He was assassinated in 1948 by a Hindu who objected to his tolerance of Muslims.
- He advocated the simple life, respect for all men, and the dignity of labor.

31

- He was a mathematician, inventor and physicist.
- This famous Greek lived 200 years B.C.
- He is quoted to have said "Eureka" when he discovered the principle relating to objects immersed in fluids.
- He invented a mechanical device (a screw that bears his name) for raising water to a higher level.
- He was the first one to determine the value of pi (π).

32

- He was a surveyor, politician and military leader.
- He is remembered for his integrity, patience and sense of duty.
- He was called the father of his country.
- He inherited several large estates, including one called Mount Vernon.
- He led American forces in fighting for independence against the British.
- He was "first in war, first in peace, first in the hearts of his countrymen."

Answers

Landmarks and Famous Sites

1. Acropolis
2. The Colosseum
3. The Eiffel Tower
4. Alamo
5. The Great Wall of China
6. Leaning Tower of Pisa
7. Lincoln Memorial
8. Pyramids of Egypt
9. Statue of Liberty
10. Taj Mahal
11. Panama Canal
12. Kremlin
13. Hanging Gardens of Babylon
14. Stonehenge
15. Tower of London
16. White House
17. Atlantis
18. Berlin Wall
19. Big Ben
20. Golden Gate Bridge
21. Sydney Opera House
22. Notre Dame
23. Machu Picchu
24. Mount Rushmore

U.S. Geography

1. Los Angeles
2. Houston
3. Lake Superior
4. Arizona
5. North Dakota
6. Virginia
7. Denver
8. Washington
9. Rio Grande River
10. Appalachian Mountains
11. Aleutian Islands
12. Mississippi
13. Massachusetts
14. Everglades National Park
15. Michigan
16. Rocky Mountains
17. New Orleans
18. Alaska
19. Tulsa
20. Texas
21. Yellowstone
22. Washington, D.C.
23. New York
24. Grand Canyon

World Geography

1. Australia
2. Brazil
3. Norway
4. Greenland
5. Sahara Desert
6. Easter Island
7. Mount Everest
8. Venice, Italy
9. Dead Sea
10. Nile River
11. Galapagos Islands
12. Saudi Arabia
13. Mexico City, Mexico
14. China
15. Chile
16. Alberta, Canada
17. Virgin Islands
18. Vienna, Austria
19. Victoria Falls
20. Tunisia
21. Tokyo, Japan
22. Tibet
23. Rome, Italy
24. The Netherlands
25. New Zealand
26. Hong Kong
27. Andes Mountains
28. Cape of Good Hope
29. Amsterdam, Netherlands
30. Beijing or Peking
31. Thailand
32. Ganges River

People

1. Mikhail Gorbachev
2. Alexander Graham Bell
3. Martin Luther King, Jr.
4. Wolfgang Mozart
5. Rembrandt
6. Benjamin Franklin
7. Thomas Jefferson
8. Abraham Lincoln
9. Neil Armstrong
10. Ludwig von Beethoven
11. Thomas Alva Edison
12. Leonardo da Vinci
13. Mao Tse-tung
14. Albert Einstein
15. Galileo
16. Charles Darwin
17. Marco Polo
18. Michelangelo
19. Florence Nightingale
20. Helen Keller
21. Alexander the Great
22. Winston Churchill
23. Marie Curie
24. Harriet Tubman
25. Lief Ericson
26. Orville and Wilbur Wright
27. John Fitzgerald Kennedy
28. Joan of Arc
29. Napoleon Bonaparte
30. Mohandas Gandhi
31. Archimedes
32. George Washington